MT. VERNON INTERMEDIATE SCHOOL

2-04
Rainbow BK
15⁹⁵

Predators in the Wild

Komodo Dragons

by Anne Welsbacher

Consultants:

The Staff of Black Hills Reptile Gardens
Rapid City, South Dakota

CAPSTONE
HIGH-INTEREST
BOOKS

an imprint of Capstone Press
Mankato, Minnesota

Capstone High-Interest Books are published by Capstone Press
151 Good Counsel Drive, P.O. Box 669, Mankato, Minnesota 56002
http://www.capstone-press.com

Library of Congress Cataloging-in-Publication Data
Welsbacher, Anne, 1955–
    Komodo dragons/by Anne Welsbacher.
    p. cm.—(Predators in the wild)
    Includes bibliographical references and index (p. 32).
    Summary: Describes the physical characteristics, habits, habitats, and
hunting methods of this giant lizard.
    ISBN 0-7368-1066-8
    1. Komodo dragon—Juvenile literature. [1. Komodo dragon. 2. Lizards.]
I. Title. II. Series.
QL666.L29 W45   2002
597.95'968—dc21   2001002928

Editorial Credits
Blake Hoena, editor; Karen Risch, product planning editor; Timothy Halldin,
    cover designer and illustrator; Katy Kudela, photo researcher

Photo Credits
Ann & Rob Simpson, 17 (bottom right)
ERH Photography/Eileen Herrling, 8, 22
Erwin and Peggy Bauer, 21
Jim Kern Expeditions, 11, 17 (bottom left)
Mark Jones/The Roving Tortoise, 12, 14, 15, 17 (top left), 20
Tui De Roy/The Roving Tortoise, 9, 16, 17 (top right), 18, 24
Wolfgang Kaehler, cover, 6, 10, 27, 28, 29

1 2 3 4 5 6 07 06 05 04 03 02

Table of Contents

Common name: Komodo dragon, Komodo monitor, ora

Scientific name: *Varqanus komodoensis*

Length: Komodo dragons grow to be more than 6 feet (1.8 meters) long. They can be as long as 10 feet (3 meters).

Weight: Most Komodo dragons grow to weigh more than 100 pounds (45 kilograms). Large Komodo dragons can weigh as much as 300 pounds (140 kilograms).

Appearance: Komodo dragons have gray or brown scales. Their scales have spots of yellow-gold. Komodo dragons have long, thick tails.

Life span: Komodo dragons can live as long as 50 years. They continue to grow larger as they age.

Habitat: Komodo dragons live on several small islands in Indonesia. Komodo dragon habitats on these islands include forests, dry grasslands, and coasts.

Prey: Komodo dragons eat deer, wild pigs, goats, snakes, fish, birds, and rodents.

Eating habits: Komodo dragons may eat more than half their weight in one meal. Komodo dragons are scavengers. They often eat dead animals.

In This Chapter:

* Komodo dragons are the world's largest lizards.

* Komodo dragons live in Indonesia.

* Young Komodo dragons live in trees.

Chapter 1

Komodo Dragons

Komodo dragons are the world's largest lizards. They grow to be more than 6 feet (1.8 meters) long. They can weigh more than 100 pounds (45 kilograms). Some of the largest Komodo dragons can grow as long as 10 feet (3 meters). They may weigh more than 300 pounds (140 kilograms).

Lizard Species

About 3,500 species of lizards exist in the world. A species is a specific type of plant or animal. Most lizards are less than 3 feet (.9 meter) long. Many of the larger lizards belong to the Varanidae family.

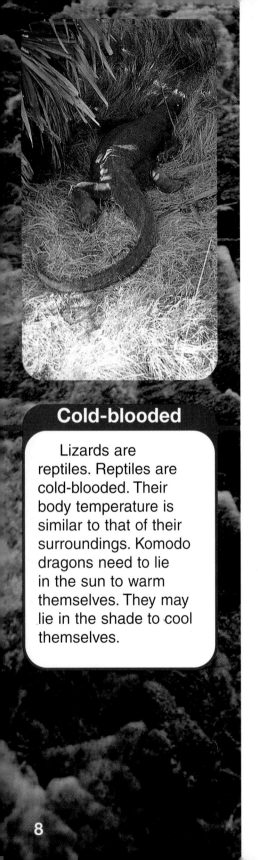

Lizards in the Varanidae family are called monitors. They have a small head, a long neck, and a long tail. People sometimes call Komodo dragons "Komodo monitors."

Appearance

Komodo dragons have gray or brown scales. They have a yellow, forked tongue. Their feet have claws that are 2 to 3 inches (5.1 to 7.6 centimeters) long.

A Komodo dragon's underbelly hangs low to the ground. After a large meal, it may even touch the ground.

Habitat

Komodo dragons live on several small islands in southeastern Indonesia. This country of islands is located between the Pacific Ocean

Cold-blooded

Lizards are reptiles. Reptiles are cold-blooded. Their body temperature is similar to that of their surroundings. Komodo dragons need to lie in the sun to warm themselves. They may lie in the shade to cool themselves.

Komodo dragons live on Komodo Island in Indonesia.

and the Indian Ocean. Komodo dragons are named after Indonesia's Komodo Island.

The islands have several types of habitats. A habitat is the place and natural conditions where an animal lives. Komodo dragon habitats include forests, dry grasslands, and coasts.

Male and female Komodo dragons are difficult to tell apart.

Mating

About three out of four Komodo dragons are male. Scientists do not know why more male Komodo dragons exist than female. But this fact makes it difficult for males to find a mate.

Male and female Komodo dragons look alike. They are difficult to tell apart. But male

Komodo dragons have a gland at the base of the tail. This organ gives off a scent. Males search for a Komodo dragon without this scent to find a female.

Komodo dragons are not social animals. They only gather in large groups when feeding. In July and August, Komodo dragons search for a mate during these gatherings.

Reproduction

Female Komodo dragons lay their eggs one month after mating. They dig a hole in which to lay their eggs. They lay 20 to 30 eggs. The eggs are about 3 inches (7.6 centimeters) long. Female Komodo dragons then cover up the hole.

In April, the eggs hatch. Hatchlings are about 18 inches (46 centimeters) long.

Hatchlings

After hatching, young Komodo dragons crawl up nearby trees. This action protects them from being eaten by adult Komodo dragons. Hatchlings eat insects, lizards, birds, and eggs that they find in trees. After about two years, Komodo dragons are too big to live in trees. They then move to the ground.

In This Chapter:

* Komodo dragons have a vomero-nasal sense.

* Komodo dragons ambush their prey.

* Komodo dragons have deadly bites.

Chapter 2

The Hunt

Komodo dragons are predators. They hunt other animals for food. Komodo dragons eat any animal that they can find and kill. Young Komodo dragons eat insects, small lizards, and birds. Adult Komodo dragons hunt deer, wild pigs, rats, chickens, and fish. They also may eat smaller Komodo dragons. Adult Komodo dragons even can kill water buffalo.

Komodo dragons also are scavengers. They eat the flesh of dead animals. This flesh is called carrion.

A Komodo dragon uses its tongue to smell.

Senses for Hunting

Scientists believe that Komodo dragons can hear and see almost as well as people can. These senses help Komodo dragons know when prey is near.

Komodo dragons have a vomero-nasal sense. This sense is a combination of smell and taste. A Komodo dragon sticks out its forked tongue to collect scent particles in the air. Its tongue then places these scent particles on the Jacobson's organ. This organ is on the roof of a Komodo dragon's mouth. A Komodo dragon can smell prey using its vomero-nasal sense. It also uses this sense to find carrion.

Hunting habits

Komodo dragons do not chase their prey. They can run only about 10 miles (16 kilometers) per hour. Many of the animals Komodo dragons hunt can outrun them. Instead, Komodo dragons ambush animals.

A Komodo dragon often finds a place in tall grass to hide. It tramples down the grass and then waits for prey to walk by. The Komodo dragon charges out at an animal when it gets close.

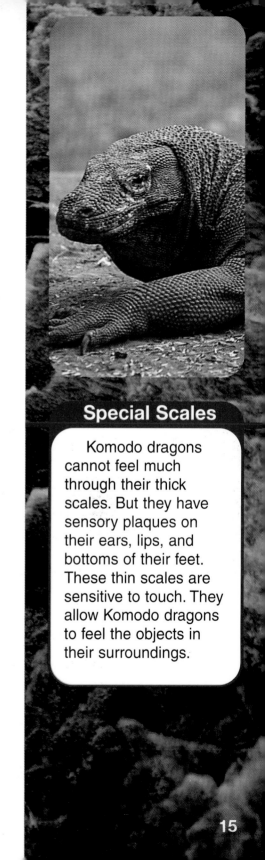

Special Scales

Komodo dragons cannot feel much through their thick scales. But they have sensory plaques on their ears, lips, and bottoms of their feet. These thin scales are sensitive to touch. They allow Komodo dragons to feel the objects in their surroundings.

A Komodo dragon's mouth is full of deadly bacteria.

Deadly Bacteria

Prey often escapes a Komodo dragon's ambush. But a Komodo dragon's bite may be enough to kill the animal. Several deadly types of bacteria live in a Komodo dragon's mouth. These tiny organisms do not harm the Komodo dragon. But the bacteria may infect an animal bitten by a Komodo dragon. The bacteria can cause blood poisoning. This illness may weaken or kill an animal.

Another type of bacteria infects the animal's wound and causes a bad smell. The Komodo dragon follows this scent to find its prey. The dying animal's scent often attracts other Komodo dragons.

What Komodo Dragons Eat

Deer

Wild Pigs

Goats

Rodents

In This Chapter:

* Komodo dragons have serrated teeth.

* Komodo dragons do not chew their food.

* Komodo dragons often eat carrion.

Chapter 3

The Kill

A Komodo dragon ambushes prey. It charges out of its hiding place when an animal passes by. A Komodo dragon often knocks its prey to the ground when it attacks. It then grabs the prey's throat and shakes the animal. This action kills the animal.

A Komodo dragon has serrated teeth. These sharp teeth have jagged edges. They easily slice through prey's flesh. A Komodo dragon's teeth also are curved toward the back of its mouth. This shape helps a Komodo dragon hold onto its prey.

Saliva

A Komodo dragon's teeth are mostly hidden by its gums. Only the tips of the teeth show. But food pushes down the gums as a Komodo dragon eats. The gums rub against the teeth and start to bleed. Blood mixes with saliva to make a pink juice. This juice allows large chunks of food to slide down the Komodo dragon's throat.

Eating Habits

A Komodo dragon bites off large chunks of meat from its prey. A Komodo dragon does not chew its food. It is able to open its mouth wide to swallow large pieces of food.

Large chunks of food often block a Komodo dragon's airway as it eats. It then uses a special tube to breathe while eating. This tube is at the back of its throat and leads to its lungs. While eating, a Komodo dragon pushes the tube out its mouth.

Digestion

A Komodo dragon eats every part of its prey. It even eats bones and hair. A Komodo dragon may eat more than half its weight in one feeding.

A Komodo dragon eats every part of its prey.

Strong acids in a Komodo dragon's stomach digest food. These chemicals break down food to be used by the body. But a Komodo dragon cannot digest every part of an animal. These parts include the teeth and horns. A Komodo dragon coughs them up in a mass called a gastric pellet.

A Komodo dragon uses its vomero-nasal sense to find carrion.

Scavenging Habits

Komodo dragons hunt for most of their food. But they seem to prefer scavenging to hunting. Finding carrion takes less energy than hunting. Komodo dragons eat any dead animals they find. They eat rotting meat. They even eat meat that is full of worms and maggots. These worm-like creatures later become flies.

Komodo dragons use their vomero-nasal sense to find carrion. Several Komodo dragons may find the same dead animal. They then circle the food and approach it carefully. Small Komodo dragons wait for the larger Komodo dragons to eat first. Large Komodo dragons might attack and kill smaller Komodo dragons. The small Komodo dragons then eat only if they sense that it is safe to do so.

Myth versus Fact

Myth: Komodo dragons are dangerous to people.

Fact: Komodo dragons have attacked people. But these attacks are rare. Only about 10 people have died from Komodo dragon attacks in the last 20 years.

Myth: Komodo dragons are actual dragons.

Fact: A Komodo dragon has a yellow tongue. In the past, people may have thought a Komodo dragon's tongue looked like fire. This led people to call them dragons.

Myth: Komodo dragons are living dinosaurs.

Fact: Komodo dragons actually descended from lizards that lived 250 million years ago.

In This Chapter:

* Komodo dragons have a small range.

* About 3,000 to 5,000 Komodo dragons exist.

* Laws protect Komodo dragons.

Chapter 4

In the World of People

Komodo dragons live in a harsh environment. Temperatures may reach 110 degrees Fahrenheit (43 degrees Celsius). Earthquakes sometimes shake the land. Giant waves sweep in from surrounding ocean waters. Fast, deep currents can drown animals that swim near the shore. Sharks swim near the islands. Many deadly snakes, scorpions, and spiders live on Komodo Island.

Yellow represents the Komodo dragon's range.

Dangers to Komodo Dragons

The biggest danger to Komodo dragons is their small population. Only 3,000 to 5,000 Komodo dragons exist in the wild. They all live in a small area. A natural disaster could kill most of them.

In the early 1980s, a large fire on Padar Island killed many Komodo dragons. The fire also killed the prey animals on the island. The surviving Komodo dragons then swam to other islands in the area. Today, no Komodo dragons live on Padar.

Komodo Island

People did not live on Komodo Island until the 1800s. The King of Indonesia sent criminals there to live as punishment. The descendants of these criminals still live on Komodo Island. Today, these people mostly are fishers.

The people on Komodo Island fear and respect Komodo dragons. They build houses on long stilts. This design prevents Komodo dragons from entering their homes. People put rocks on graves. This action keeps Komodo dragons from digging up and eating the dead bodies.

Today, many people visit Komodo Island. Tourists come to see Komodo dragons. Scientists come to study Komodo dragons.

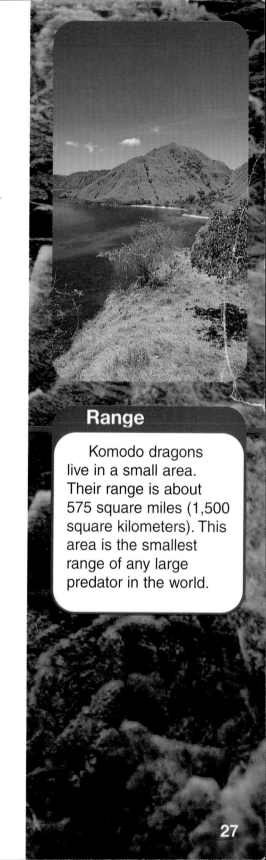

Range

Komodo dragons live in a small area. Their range is about 575 square miles (1,500 square kilometers). This area is the smallest range of any large predator in the world.

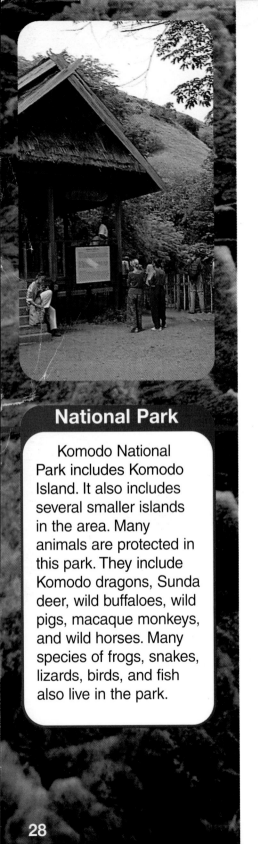

National Park

Komodo National Park includes Komodo Island. It also includes several smaller islands in the area. Many animals are protected in this park. They include Komodo dragons, Sunda deer, wild buffaloes, wild pigs, macaque monkeys, and wild horses. Many species of frogs, snakes, lizards, birds, and fish also live in the park.

Survival

Komodo dragons are considered endangered. Scientists believe Komodo dragons are in danger of dying out because few of them exist. A disaster similar to Padar Island's fire could kill most of the Komodo dragon population.

The government of Indonesia is trying to protect Komodo dragons and their habitat. In 1928, Komodo Island become a protected wilderness area. In 1980, the Indonesian government made Komodo Island a national park. It now is illegal to hurt or kill Komodo dragons.

Zoos also are helping to keep Komodo dragons from dying out. In 1992, the first Komodo dragon hatched in captivity. It hatched at the

Komodo dragons are protected in Komodo National Park.

National Zoo in Washington, D.C. Today, about 50 Komodo dragons live in zoos across North America. These animals will help make sure that Komodo dragons continue to exist in the world.

ambush (AM-bush)—to hide and then attack; Komodo dragons ambush their prey.

carrion (KARE-ee-uhn)—dead animal flesh

digest (dye-JEST)—to break down food so that it can be used by the body

habitat (HAB-uh-tat)—the place and natural conditions in which a plant or an animal lives

plaque (PLAK)—a flat, thin covering

predator (PRED-uh-tur)—an animal that hunts other animals for food

range (RAYNJ)—an area where an animal mostly lives

scavenger (SKAV-uhn-jer)—an animal that eats carrion

social (SOH-shuhl)—living in groups or packs; Komodo dragons are not social animals.

species (SPEE-sheez)—a specific type of animal or plant

vomero-nasal sense (VAH-meh-ro NAY-zuhl SENSS)—a sense that allows some animals to smell with their tongue

To Learn More

Darling, Kathy. *Komodo Dragon.* On Location. New York: Lothrop, Lee, & Shepard Books, 1997.

Martin, James. *Komodo Dragons: Giant Lizards of Indonesia.* Animals & the Environment. Mankato, Minn.: Capstone Books, 1995.

Miller, Geoff. *Komodo Dragons.* Nature's Children. Danbury, Conn.: Grolier Educational, 1999.

Useful Addresses

Black Hills Reptile Gardens
P.O. Box 620
Rapid City, SD 57709

Komodo National Park Foundation
P.O. Box 195
Ubud Bali 80571
Indonesia

Smithsonian National Zoological Park
3001 Connecticut Avenue N.W.
Washington, DC 20008

Woodland Park Zoo
5500 Phinney Avenue North
Seattle, WA 98103-5897

Internet Sites

Animal Fact Sheets–Komodo Dragon

http://www.zoo.org/educate/fact_sheets/
  kom_dragon/komodo.htm

Black Hills Reptile Gardens

http://www.reptile-gardens.com

Scientific American–The Komodo Dragon

http://www.sciam.com/1999/0399issue/
  0399ciofi.html

Index

DATE DUE
